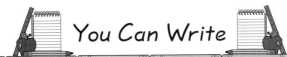
Jan 06

AEA

$16.95

You Can Write a Report

Jennifer Rozines Roy

Enslow Publishers, Inc.

40 Industrial Road   PO Box 38
Box 398   Aldershot
Berkeley Heights, NJ 07922   Hants GU12 6BP
USA   UK

http://www.enslow.com

Library of Congress Cataloging-in-Publication Data

Roy, Jennifer Rozines.
    You can write a report / Jennifer Rozines Roy.
       v. cm. — (You can write)
    Includes bibliographical references (p.) and index.
    Contents: You can write a report — Reports—what's in them — Getting
started — Getting the right stuff in the right order — It's time to
write! — The finishing touches.
    ISBN 0-7660-2086-X (hardcover)
    1. Report writing—Juvenile literature. [1. Report writing.] I.
Title. II. Series.
    LB1047.3 .R694 2002
    808'.02—dc21
                                2002008402

Printed in the United States of America

10 9 8 7 6 5 4 3 2

Illustration Credits: Enslow Publishers, Inc.

Cover: Enslow Publishers, Inc.

Table of Contents

1 You Can Write a Report 5

2 Reports—What's in Them 11

3 Getting Started 19

4 Getting the Right Stuff in
the Right Order 30

5 It's Time to Write! 41

6 The Finishing Touches 51

A Sample Student
Research Report 58

Glossary 62

Further Reading and
Internet Addresses 63

Index 64

Chapter One

You Can Write a Report

Y ou sit at your desk staring at a blank piece of paper. Ever since your teacher gave you the assignment to write a report, you have procrastinated, worried, and complained. But you have not written a word. The deadline is looming, and you are starting to feel a panic attack coming on. *How will you hand in your paper by the due date if you cannot even get started?*

There is something about writing reports that makes some students nervous. They may think it is too difficult or confusing or even boring. It is true that report writing takes time and effort. But believe it or not, it can be enjoyable and exciting too.

Maybe this is your first time writing a report, and you have not really been taught how to do it. Or perhaps you have had a lousy experience in the past and want to make it better this time. Well, this book can help. It will give you the tools to write a successful report, taking you step-by-step through the research and writing processes. By the time you are finished, you will have the knowledge, the skills, and the confidence to write a terrific report. The good news is, you just may have fun along the way.

Why Do You Need to Know How to Write a Report?

First of all, it is important for school. You will probably have to do reports for many of your classes. Doing a good job may mean getting good grades and passing the class. But even after you graduate, you still may have to write reports for your job. Businesspeople, engineers, doctors, scientists, teachers, psychologists, and journalists are just some of the people who use research and report writing skills for their careers.

The rewards of writing a good report, however, are more than just a grade or paycheck. Learning about something that interests you, working hard and completing a project, and sharing the results with others will give you pride and satisfaction.

What Is a Report?

A report is a gathering of information about a subject. It tells people facts and details and presents its findings in an interesting way. A good report is based on solid research. In a report, you

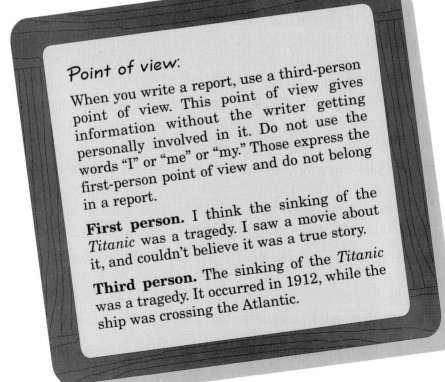

Point of view:

When you write a report, use a third-person point of view. This point of view gives information without the writer getting personally involved in it. Do not use the words "I" or "me" or "my." Those express the first-person point of view and do not belong in a report.

First person. I think the sinking of the *Titanic* was a tragedy. I saw a movie about it, and couldn't believe it was a true story.

Third person. The sinking of the *Titanic* was a tragedy. It occurred in 1912, while the ship was crossing the Atlantic.

ZZZ ... Wake me up when a boring report is over!

should try to stick mainly to the facts. Facts can be proven. They make a report accurate and strong.

Sometimes it is appropriate to include your own feelings or opinions in a report. For example, you may be writing your report to support an opinion you have. Perhaps you think that too much homework is bad for kids. In your report, you would have to find research to back that up. But however you feel about your subject, it is important to present your report in a matter-of-fact manner, using the third-person point of view.

A good report is well organized, presenting the information in an order that makes it easy to understand. A report should also be well written.

Make writing more fun:

Write about things that interest you. If you think your topic (what your report is about) is exciting, you will enjoy researching and writing a lot more. Even if your topic is assigned, such as "America in the nineteenth century," your teacher may let you choose an aspect that appeals to you—pioneer children, for example, or a slave's daring escape to freedom.

Make it splash! Except for illustrations, you may need to stick with black ink on white paper for your final report. But if you're the only one who will see your research notes or rough draft, why not go nuts? Funky note paper, different colored inks . . . whatever!

Take a breather. Stressed out? Stuck? Try a five-minute jog, dance around to your favorite song, or just close your eyes and clear your mind. You'll come back to work refreshed and ready to go.

Work in a group. Unless your friends will distract you, get together and cheer each other on.

Plan something special for when your report is done. Ice cream? A movie? A long nap? Then sharpen your pencil, turn on your computer, and get to it. The sooner you start, the sooner you'll get your special treat!

When writing your report, try to use words and sentences that make it clear and interesting. An effective report tells the reader about something *and* keeps his or her attention from beginning to end. You do not want your audience dozing off during your report.

Finally, when all the planning, researching, and writing is complete, a report is presented to others. It might be typed on paper and read by your teacher or boss or community. It could be read aloud to your class as an oral report. However the results are shared, the last step of the report writing process is to let other people know what you have found out. This is the moment all of your hard work gets recognized, and you can pat yourself on the back and say, "I did it! I wrote a great report!"

Chapter Two

Reports—What's in Them

People write reports for different reasons. Before you write your report, think about its purpose. This will help you decide which type to write. Do you want to share information about something you have learned? Have you performed an experiment and need to present the results? Did you read a book and want to tell others about it? Or do you want to report on events that just happened?

There are different types of reports for all these different purposes. The type of report you write—and the words you use in it—can also depend on your audience. Who will be reading or listening to your report? A teacher who assigns a written science report may require a lab report with detailed results and scientific vocabulary. However, if you are presenting a book report aloud to your classmates, you will probably use a more informal tone and express your opinion in your own words.

Research Report

A research report is the most common type of report students have to do for school. Research reports take information from different places (called sources) and present it in an organized paper. Research reports mostly discuss facts and thoughts that other people have written about.

For example, if you want to know about Martin Luther King, Jr., or the history of snowboarding, you would look up information about your subject. You might use library books, newspaper and magazine articles, and the Internet. (Find out from your teacher what kinds of sources are acceptable for the assignment.) Then you would write your report based on what you found from the various sources.

Hey, can I help?

First you do the research. Then you report it. Research report . . . get it?

Investigative Report

Another type of research report investigates and tests a problem or question. It might include research using published sources, but it also adds one important thing—your own original research. For this kind of report, you will have to collect data or conduct an experiment and present the findings. For example, let's say you want to know how many students in your school have tried smoking cigarettes. First you could research student smoking in books and magazines and on the Internet. That would give you the review of literature to write up. Then you could do a survey of your classmates. That would give you the firsthand information to answer your original question.

Lab Report

If you have a scientific question, you may want to conduct an experiment. Perhaps you are curious about how different conditions affect plant growth. Or you want to know which skin cleanser clears up acne best. Sure, you could find out what others have discovered in similar research in the past. That would be good for the section that discusses information you have found in research sources. However, doing your own experiment gives you the chance to test your ideas and prove the results. So you would perform the experiment, write up your findings, and share them in your lab report. Just make sure you follow all safety procedures for the experiment and get an adult's permission first.

Book Report

A book report is another type of report that teachers assign. A book report discusses a book that you have read. It is different from a research report, because it gives you the opportunity to give your opinion along with facts. A book report tells what the book is about and may include background information about the subject of the book and the book's author. You may choose a book you really enjoyed, one that you feel is important, or even one that you did not like at all. After you describe it, you can tell whether you recommend it or not—and why.

News Report

There is a type of report you may see every day on television or read in the newspaper. News reports inform an audience about events that are going on in the world. To write a news report, you gather up-to-date facts and present them to readers or listeners.

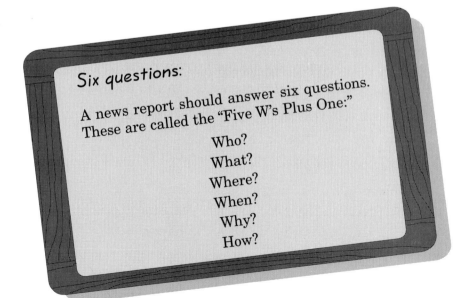

Six questions:

A news report should answer six questions. These are called the "Five W's Plus One:"

Who?
What?
Where?
When?
Why?
How?

These are just some of the different types of reports students learn to write. Whether you have to do a research report, a news report, or a book report, your job as a writer is to make it clear, informative, and interesting. You may find one particular type of report easier or more enjoyable, but chances are you will have to write at least one of each type sometime in your life.

They all sound fun. I think I'll write one of each!

Types of Reports:
1. Research report
2. Investigative report
3. Lab report
4. Book report

The Parts of a Report

All reports have at least three basic parts—an introduction, a body, and a conclusion. A research report must also show where that research came from. A list of sources usually goes at the end of the report. Sources of specific facts, quotes, and ideas are also identified within the report itself. You will learn how to do these steps later in the book.

Introduction

The introduction is a paragraph that starts the report. It introduces the topic, which is the subject you are writing about. The introduction also gives a statement, called a thesis statement, that tells the main idea of your paper.

The introduction is written in a way that makes the audience want to know more. A good introduction grabs the audience's attention and sets the stage for more interesting things to come. For example, read the following introductions. Which one does a better job of getting your attention and making you want to read more?

> #1—"Leeches are skinny, segmented worms. They have disks that inhale blood. Used by old-fashioned doctors for hundreds of years to remove toxins from the body, leeches are now making a comeback in modern medicine."

> #2—"They are skinny. They are slimy. They are bloodthirsty creatures who have no faces. This may sound like something from a horror movie, but it is actually a description of a small animal that has helped doctors for hundreds of years. Leeches are segmented worms with sucking disks that, when used properly, can remove toxins from the human body. Long considered old-fashioned and unnecessary, leeches are now making a comeback in modern medicine."

Introduction #2 is the better choice. It instantly draws the reader in with its more interesting choice of words.

Body

The body is the middle section of the report. The body includes a number of paragraphs that present the information and findings. Every paragraph in the body is about the main topic, but each one explains a different point.

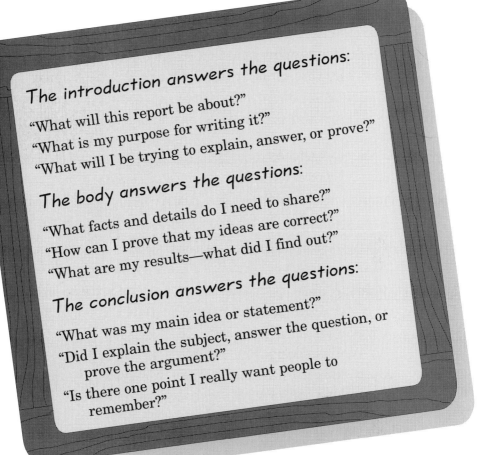

The introduction answers the questions:

"What will this report be about?"

"What is my purpose for writing it?"

"What will I be trying to explain, answer, or prove?"

The body answers the questions:

"What facts and details do I need to share?"

"How can I prove that my ideas are correct?"

"What are my results—what did I find out?"

The conclusion answers the questions:

"What was my main idea or statement?"

"Did I explain the subject, answer the question, or prove the argument?"

"Is there one point I really want people to remember?"

Conclusion

The conclusion is the paragraph that wraps everything up. A strong conclusion makes the audience feel satisfied that the writer presented a complete and effective report. The conclusion may state the main idea one last time, give a summary of the most important points, and give some last thoughts about the topic.

List of Sources

A research report includes an alphabetical list of sources at the end, usually appearing on its own page. It tells which books, magazines, newspaper articles, Web sites, or other sources you used for information about your topic.

There are two main approaches to doing this kind of list. Typically, a bibliography includes all of the sources you consulted, even if you did not end up using information from all of them. A list of works cited includes only those sources you actually took information from. Be careful, though—some people use these words differently. Make sure you know which approach your teacher prefers. Either way, however, there are specific ways of preparing the list. This will be covered later in the book.

Why is such a list required? It shows that you used enough different sources for your research. It shows that the sources you chose are appropriate and reliable. It also gives enough information that if someone else wanted to look up more stuff about your topic, they could find the sources you used. Finally, it gives credit where credit is due. When ideas or information comes from someone else's work, it is important to give them proper credit for it.

Can you say the word "bibliography" ten times fast?

Chapter Three

Getting Started

So now you know all about the different kinds of reports and what they contain. It must be time to sit down and write one, right? Not so fast! There are some things you must do before you write. This is called the *prewriting stage*. Remember, the prewriting planning you do now will make it much easier to write your report later.

The prewriting process includes choosing a topic, doing research, taking notes, writing a thesis statement, and creating an outline. This chapter and the next will take you through all of these prewriting steps, beginning with the question *"What is your report about?"* With all the many things to write about, how do you decide on a topic?

Choosing a Topic

The topic is the main subject of a report.

Sometimes a teacher will assign the topic for you. While in this case you do not have the choice about *what* to write, you still get to make your report as interesting as you possibly can. Many times, however, you will be responsible for choosing your own topic. There are steps you can take to make sure the topic you select is just right for your report.

First, decide on a general subject area. Make sure the subject interests you and is appropriate for the class.

Now focus your topic. If it is too general, there will be too much information to pack into one report. If the topic is too narrow or specific, there will not be enough information for a complete

Hot topics:
- ✔ The environment
- ✔ Current events affecting your community or school
- ✔ Health concerns
- ✔ Scientific breakthroughs
- ✔ Famous people
- ✔ Issues that affect teens
- ✔ Books by minorities and women
- ✔ Unusual hobbies or activities
- ✔ Historical events told from a unique perspective

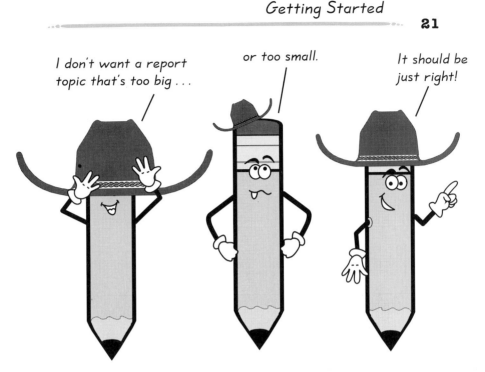

report. Do a preliminary search on your topic by skimming reference books or the Internet. This will help you see how much information is available. Once you are satisfied with your choice, check in with your teacher to make sure it is acceptable and fits the assignment.

If you are having some trouble coming up with a topic, you may try a "topic cluster." This is a graphic organizer that lets you map out your thoughts, placing a general topic in the center and brainstorming specific ideas for the branches. Once the cluster is drawn, you will have a better idea of what idea interests you *and* has the right amount of information for your report.

Temporary Thesis Statement

After you have selected your topic, you need to develop a temporary thesis statement. A thesis

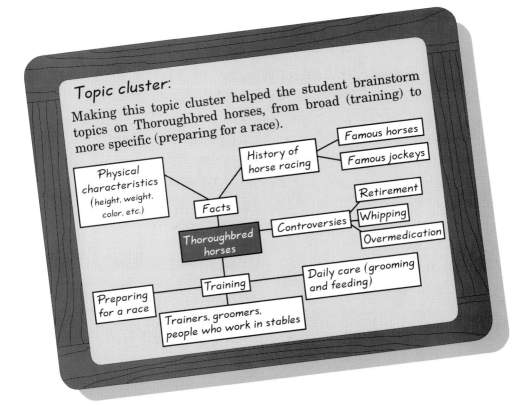

Topic cluster:
Making this topic cluster helped the student brainstorm topics on Thoroughbred horses, from broad (training) to more specific (preparing for a race).

statement is one sentence that tells the main point or argument you will make in your paper.

"But how am I supposed to know what my main point is when I have not done my research?" you may ask. The answer: You're not. That's where the word *temporary* comes in. Nothing is final here. At this point, you are just making a guess about what you *think* you will discover or prove. You may change your temporary thesis statement at any time during your research. For now, however, it gives you a good starting point and sets you off in the right direction for your research.

The Research

There are many, many places to find facts and details about your topic. These places are called reference sources. Primary reference sources are eyewitness accounts or original documents. Letters, diaries, and personal interviews are primary sources. Secondary sources take their information from somewhere else. Magazines, books, and Internet articles are examples of secondary sources.

It is up to you to decide which sources offer you the best research information. To help you evaluate your source, ask yourself the following three questions. If you can answer "yes" to all of

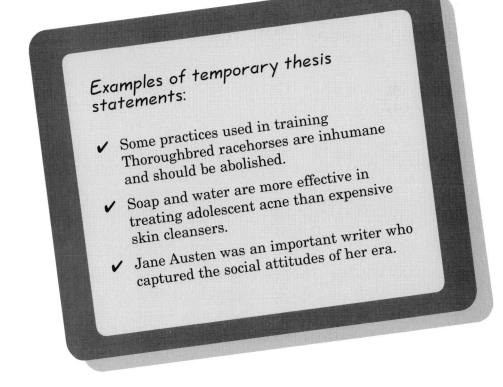

Examples of temporary thesis statements:

✔ Some practices used in training Thoroughbred racehorses are inhumane and should be abolished.

✔ Soap and water are more effective in treating adolescent acne than expensive skin cleansers.

✔ Jane Austen was an important writer who captured the social attitudes of her era.

them, you will know you have found a good source for your report.

1. Is this information useful? You cannot include everything you find in every book or article about your topic. Only use information that gives you facts, details, and opinions that relate directly to your report. Your goal is to support (or contradict) your thesis statement—not fill pages about everything everyone has ever said about your topic.

2. Is the material up-to-date? Whenever you find a source that you plan to use, be sure to check the date that it was published. Knowledge and ideas change over time. Therefore, try to find the most recent information available. It takes a while for books to be printed and information to be kept current. Although older books and articles may be accurate, your best bet is usually to use newer published sources. One advantage of researching over the Internet is that the information can be updated more easily. Online documents and sites usually list the original date of publication, and then note newer dates if the material was revised. Look over these dates to determine whether the online information is current or outdated.

3. Is the source reliable? This is important. Not all sources are accurate or trustworthy.

Sometimes the person who wrote the information you have found has certain beliefs or prejudices about the topic. An author who uses emotional language, presents only one side of an issue, or makes unproven or inaccurate statements will not give you solid research. Of course, many writers have an opinion about their subject. It is when their opinions get in the way of the accuracy or believability of their writing that the source becomes unreliable.

How do you evaluate a source for reliability? After all, you are a student doing a report—not an expert. A good way to evaluate a resource is by checking the sources the author used. Look over the list of works cited. A good list has titles that are reputable, balanced, and up-to-date. Something else you can do is use books by well-known publishers and articles from magazines with good reputations. Another helpful method is to look up the author's background. Does the author have the education, expertise, or experience to write knowledgeably about the topic? Perhaps you could even find some reviews of the source and see what other experts think about this author and his or her writing.

Internet Sources

Be extra careful about using information from the Internet. It is safest to use sites published by respected organizations (.org), educational institutions (.edu), and government agencies

Plagiarizing is no joke! Even a funny guy like me takes it seriously.

Remember, you absolutely must give proper credit when you use information. Copying someone else's words or ideas and pretending they are your own is called plagiarizing. Plagiarizing is illegal. It is stealing someone else's work. Plagiarizing can get you a flunking grade or even get you expelled. It is a serious matter, so be careful to use your own words and ideas or show where you got the information. Writing the source of each note on your card will help ensure that you give credit where credit is due.

The notes you take will either *paraphrase* or *quote* the information you find. To paraphrase, write down what you have read using your own words. To quote, copy the information word for word. Then, put quotation marks around the quotes. You can quote a sentence or a whole paragraph. Try not to use too many quotations in your report. You want to show plenty of original thinking and writing.

Examples:

Paraphrase: Horse owner Amy Lexus thinks that training methods are kinder to animals than they used to be.

Quote: "Current training practices are much more compassionate than they were in the past." —horse owner Amy Lexus.

If your quote is several lines long, you may

need to set it off in a block quotation. To do this, begin a new line, indenting about one inch from the left margin. Even though it is a direct quote, you do not have to use quotation marks for a block quotation. It will be clear from the way it is indented.

Example of a block quotation:

> Most schoolchildren who have been bullied feel unsafe long after the bullying incident. Bullies threaten more vulnerable children with future violence, which makes the victim feel almost constant apprehension and insecurity. Although kids have always had conflicts, these days bullies are much more apt to escalate into rougher and more violent behavior.

After you have gone through all your reference sources and taken the notes you need from each, look through your cards. Do you have enough information for your report? Are there any leftover gaps or questions you have? If you answered "yes," go back to the library or computer and continue your research. If you answered "no," your research of materials is complete.

Doing Your Own Research

You have gathered information from primary and secondary sources. But what about your own research? If you need original findings—ones you discover yourself—it is time to collect some data. Doing your own research is fun, but keeping your data organized is tricky. Here's how!

Data is specific, factual information that can

Show validity and reliability. Collect your data to the best of your ability. Then you can be a good researcher, just like me!

help you support your thesis statement. When you record and report your data, it is important to be careful and accurate.

The method of collecting data you choose must have validity and reliability. *Validity* means that you are really measuring what you say you are measuring. For example, suppose you are testing the amount of rainfall in your backyard. You accidentally leave the rain collector underneath a gutter that drips. The water drips get mixed in with the raindrops. Therefore, your test is not valid.

Reliability means that someone else could follow your steps exactly and get similar results. To show that your data is reliable, you should write down what you do in detail. That way, anyone could do a retest and see that your procedure was reliable.

Surveys

One method of gathering data is by doing a survey. To conduct a survey, the researcher asks a question or questions to a group of people. The survey can be done by written questionnaire or by asking face-to-face or over the phone.

Let's say you want to find out the most popular school lunch. You could survey your classmates face-to-face and write down their answers. Or you could hand out questionnaires that ask students to write in a vote for their favorite lunch along with any comments.

Experiments

Experiments are also a good way to collect data. An experiment is a controlled procedure carried out to discover, test, or demonstrate something.

When conducting an experiment, write down everything you use. These are called the materials. List the number and amounts in detail so that your materials list is very clear. Now perform your experiment. Write down everything you did, step-by-step. This is called your method. Finally, record your data. All of these notes will be very helpful when you write your report.

You may want to display your data in a table or graph. A table helps to organize your

Table

President's Physical Fitness Award Qualifications

Age	1-mile run (minutes:seconds)	Pull-ups
Boys		
10	7:57	6
11	7:32	6
12	7:11	7
Girls		
10	9:19	2
11	9:02	2
12	8:23	3

information in rows (that go across) and columns (that go down). Write a title above your chart to tell what results it shows.

Graphs are pictures of data that use bars, shapes, or lines to show results. Some types of graphs are line graphs, bar graphs, and pie graphs. Visual displays of your findings will help you see patterns and make judgments about your research.

Take a look at your results. Are they the results you expected? Sometimes an experiment will prove that your temporary thesis statement was right. Other times, it will show something else. Do not change your data even if things do not turn out the way you thought they would. The purpose of an experiment is to discover the answer to a question. No matter what the answer turns out to be, write down the results exactly.

Oops! My research showed something different than I'd thought. I'll have to change my thesis statement. Good thing I have a big eraser...

The Final Thesis Statement

Remember back at the beginning of the prewriting stage, when you came up with a statement that you thought would sum up your report? Now that you have taken your notes and discovered results, look back at that temporary thesis statement. Do you still agree with it? If your research supports it, keep it. If the things you have learned since you wrote it have made you change your mind, write a new thesis statement.

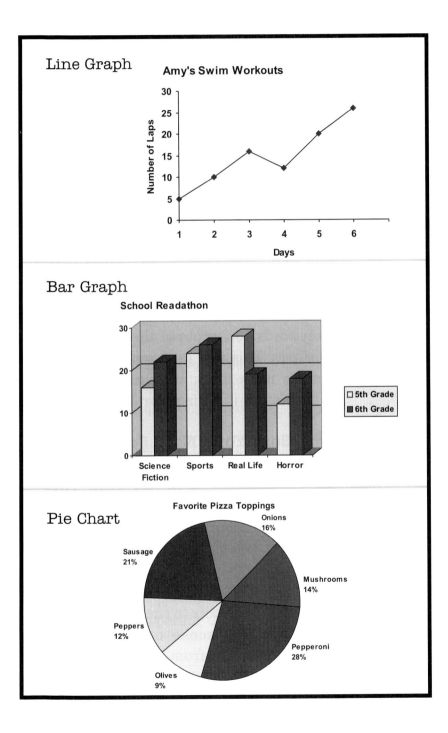

Line Graph

Amy's Swim Workouts

Bar Graph

School Readathon

Pie Chart

Favorite Pizza Toppings

thoughts about your topic. Try to leave the audience satisfied that you proved your point. Wrap up your report with confidence.

The list of sources and any other additional pages (like survey forms or data charts) go at the end of your report.

Book Report

Write the introduction. Give the title and author and a few sentences that introduce the book.

In the body, give facts and details about the book. If it is fiction, tell about the characters (people) and setting (time and place). Discuss the plot (action in the story), but be sure you do not give away the ending. If the book is nonfiction, explain what kind of book it is (biography, travel, history, science, etc.). Give some information that was included in the book.

You may want to share your opinion about the book. What did you think of it? Why? Give examples to explain why you feel this way. Be specific. Describe scenes that surprised, scared, or excited you. Offer a quote by a character that made you laugh or groan. Discuss ideas or themes that made you think. Be sure to mention how the book made you feel. Did it touch your heart, motivate you to do something new, or cause you to feel sad?

After you have covered everything you want your audience to know, write your conclusion. Wrap up the main points. Tell why you would or would not encourage others to read this book.

News Report

Write the introduction with an attention-grabbing "lead." Try to make the audience interested right away.

My body contains facts and details too!

The body includes facts and details that are up-to-date. If your story is about current events, give some background about the people and places involved. For a human interest story (one about everyday people's lives), offer information that makes the audience feel as if they want to know those people. A sports report should contain scores, highlights, and details about the athletes that made the game interesting.

Your conclusion should be brief and to the point. A sentence or two that retells the main idea of the story will complete the news report.

Document Your Sources

In addition to your final bibliography or list of works cited, you will be giving credit to your reference sources throughout your paper. Each time you include specific information from another source—a fact, a quote, or another person's idea—you will identify which source and which page that information came from.

There are several ways of doing this. Some teachers prefer in-text citations, which sound difficult but are pretty easy to work with. This is the method we will concentrate on in this book. Other teachers prefer footnotes or endnotes. You have probably seen this method used in books. It

Glossary

audience—The people who read or hear what you have written.

body—The writing between the introduction and conclusion that develops the main idea.

brainstorming—Gathering ideas by thinking about all of the possibilities.

data—Information (such as facts, figures, and examples) from which conclusions can be drawn.

draft—A piece of writing not in its final form.

graphic organizer—A display of ideas.

introduction—The beginning of the report.

prewriting—The planning stage before writing.

quote—To use someone else's words directly.

report—A piece of writing that results from researching and organizing facts about a topic.

revise—To change writing so that it is improved.

source—A reference for information.

thesis statement—A sentence that tells the purpose or main idea.

topic—The main idea.

works cited page—A list of the sources used in a report.

Further Reading

Books

Baugh, L. Sue. *How to Write Term Papers and Reports*. Chicago: VGM Career Horizons, 1997.

Elliott, Rebecca S. and James. *Painless Research Projects*. Hauppauge, N.Y.: Barron's Educational Series, 1998.

James, Elizabeth, and Carol Barkin. *How to Write Super School Reports*. New York: Lothrop, Lee & Shepard, 1998.

Strunk, William Jr., and E.B. White. *The Elements of Style*. 3rd ed. New York: Macmillan, 1979.

Internet Addresses

Kids Online Magazine

<http://www.kidsonlinemagazine.com/writingtips.html>

Writing a Book Report

<http://www.webspawner.com/users/BBBookReport>

Writing-World.com

<http://www.writing-world.com>

Index

A

audience, 10, 14

B

bibliography, 18, 28, 48–50

binding, 54–55

body, 15, 16, 17

book reports, 14, 44

brainstorming, 21

C

computer effects, 52–53

conclusion, 15, 17

cover, 54–55

D

data collection, 33–36

drafts, 41–43, 47–48, 50

E

editing, 47–48

experiments, 35–36

F

final draft, 48, 50

first draft, 41–43

first person, 7

formats, 43–45

G

graphic organizers, 21

graphics, 52–53

graphs, 36, 37, 52

I

illustrations, 52–53

Internet, 24, 25–26, 27, 55–56

introduction, 15–16, 17

investigative reports, 13

L

lab reports, 13

N

news reports, 14–15, 45

note taking, 31–34

O

oral reports, 56–57

outline, 38–40

P

plagiarizing, 32, 56

presentation, 55–57

prewriting, 19, 40

primary sources, 28–29

proofreading, 47–48

publishing, 51, 55–57

Q

quotations, 32–33, 41–42

R

Reader's Guide to Periodical Literature, 27

reference sources, 12, 18, 23–29, 45–47, 48–50

reliability, 34

research process, 23–29

research reports, 12, 18, 43–44

revision, 47

S

sample report, 58–61

sources, 12, 18, 23–29, 45–47, 48–50

surveys, 34–35

T

tables, 35, 36, 52

thesis statement, 15, 21–22, 23, 36, 38

third person, 7

title page, 51–52

topic, 9, 15, 18, 19–21

V

validity, 34

W

Web sites, 24, 25–26, 27, 50, 55–56

works cited page, 18, 25, 28–29, 45, 48–50

writing process, 41–43